Chakras

A Comprehensive Meditation Guide For Novices To Facilitate The Harmonization Of Chakras In Pursuit Of Well-Being And Contentment

(An Informative Resource On Exploring, Releasing, And Harmonizing Your Chakras)

Julian Chandler

TABLE OF CONTENT

Reestablishing Equilibrium Within The Solar Plexus Chakra.

The solar plexus chakra, also known as manipura in Sanskrit, represents the third energy center within the human body. The hue of this object is yellow and it is intricately linked with the element of 'fire'. Additionally, it bears the symbol indicated below.

What is the function and purpose of the solar plexus chakra?

Frequently denoted as the 'resplendent jewel', the third chakra is situated within the gastric vicinity, precisely at the pinnacle of the abdominal domain. It pertains to the notions of one's self-worth and self-perception, particularly in relation to one's position within the broader worldly context. Additionally, it assumes responsibility for your self-control, capacity for empathy and pardon, aptitude for deriving lessons from challenges and obstacles encountered, self-sufficiency, and aptitude for discerning one's life's calling. It additionally regulates the functioning of your abdominal region and the process of digestion.

What are the consequences of an open or blocked Solar Plexus Chakra?

When the third chakra is unblocked, an individual possesses a robust sense of self-worth, experiences a positive self-perception, and exhibits the bravery required to pursue their genuine desires. Furthermore, you maintain a sense of assuredness, self-restraint, and self-mastery over your impulses, while also manifesting kindness towards both yourself and others. You exhibit a remarkable ability to relinquish and reflect upon your missteps, thereby deriving valuable insights that pave the way for personal growth and success. Furthermore, your gastrointestinal system and abdominal functions operate optimally, resulting in a sense of well-being and contentment.

In contrast, when this pathway is obstructed, individuals may experience difficulties in maintaining a positive self-image and may view themselves as lacking in competence and value. Additionally, you encounter difficulties in discerning your life's purpose and lead a life devoid of meaning. Additionally, there is a high probability that you will dwell on past events excessively and struggle to move past them, finding it difficult to let go of the distressing encounters.

Furthermore, you experience gastrointestinal spasms, abdominal distension, queasiness, and cognitive impairments. If you find that these issues endure in your life, it is advisable to implement the subsequent strategies with the aim of rejuvenating your third chakra.

Methods for Restoring and Balancing Your Solar Plexus Chakra

Commence by adopting any of the ensuing practices and gradually integrate all of them into your daily regimen with the aim of restoring balance and vitality to your third chakra.

Crystal Healing

It is advisable to carry yellow-hued gemstones, such as Amber, Citrine, and Yellow Tourmaline, on your person at all times. Please ensure that you position the item on your nightstand and hold it for a duration of 10 minutes on a daily basis. Alternatively, you may choose to store it beneath your pillow or within your bag, or even adorn yourself with jewelry crafted from these stones in order to reap the benefits they offer.

Meditative Technique

Assume a comfortable sitting position and commence by engaging in deep inhalations and exhalations. Direct your focus towards your abdominal region and envision a gentle, luminous sphere emitting a warm, yellow radiance within your upper abdomen. Envision the circular object emitting a radiant and amplified glow, expanding to encompass the entirety of your physical form. Imagine it rotating in a clockwise direction and expanding from your body, imbuing you with feelings of joy and security. Engage in a regular regimen of practicing this exercise for a duration of 10 minutes, two times per day, in order to rejuvenate vitality and restore equilibrium to the third chakra.

Eat Right

Incorporate yellow-hued food items into your daily dietary intake, such as yellow peppers, cantaloupes, lemons, melons, mangoes, corn, and squashes. Furthermore, incorporate nourishing complex carbohydrates such as wholegrain cereal and brown rice into your dietary regimen to enhance the vitality of your solar plexus chakra. The consumption of chamomile tea on a daily basis has been found to induce a soothing and calming effect on the third chakra.

Affirmations

The subsequent assertions recited with assurance and tranquility serve to reinstate equilibrium within the third chakra as well:

I possess a strong sense of self-worth and experience immense satisfaction with regards to my personal identity.

I emanate a aura of confidence and tranquility in all my interactions.

I am experiencing a sense of strength, empowerment, and contentment.

I am deserving of all the positive opportunities and rewards that the cosmos has in store.

I possess a strong sense of empathy and am inclined to grant forgiveness, both towards myself and others.

Integrate the Fire Element into Your Daily Regimen

The act of immersing oneself in the proximity of a hearth or a bonfire imparts a pleasant sensation of warmth to the solar plexus chakra, thereby invoking a state of equilibrium within it. Additionally, partake in alternative pursuits pertaining to the elemental force of fire, such as culinary endeavors, kindling a hearth, and analogous undertakings.

Consistent implementation of these practices on a daily basis contributes to a state of equilibrium and overall contentment. In order to foster the expansion of positive energy, it is advisable to focus on nurturing and restoring your fourth chakra.

How To Achieve Equilibrium Within The Throat Chakra

Apply gentle pressure to the muscles of the neck and jaw. Consume your food in a deliberate and cautious manner. Rinse or gargle with a warm saline solution. Consume warm herbal tea. Breathe with intention. Employ frequent pauses during one's discourse. Listen to others. Practice silent contemplation of thoughts without expressing them verbally. When experiencing anger, engage in a process of numerical enumeration until such time that the intensity of said emotion diminishes. Refrain from engaging in discourse regarding negative matters. Engage in the practice of recording thoughts and experiences within a personal journal. Dispatch a written correspondence, i.e., a letter, postcard, or electronic mail. Maintain a daily practice of silence.

Practice early-morning automatic writing. Meditate. Adhere to a personal commitment to remain silent. Laugh. Engage in vocal performance, vocalize rhythmically, or recite audibly. Communicate with sincerity and benevolence. Engage in a type of artistic pursuit. Engage in artistic activities such as sketching, painting, expressing through colors, or constructing. Enroll in a course focused on improving public speaking skills. Acquire proficiency in a foreign language. Please attempt the subsequent yoga asanas: forward fold, upward-facing dog, camel posture, bridge pose.

THE THIRD EYE

Amidst the eyebrows, hues of indigo and purple conjure intuition.

A state of equilibrium in the third eye chakra engenders a comprehensive perception and an overall sense of tranquility. It bestows upon an individual the capacity for intuitive and perceptive discernment in their ordinary existence, along with the visual stimulus necessary to transcend it. The development of impressive creativity and visual abilities frequently stems from the lucidity one acquires. The ability to retrieve memories and dreams is indicative of equilibrium as well.

An imbalance of energy is linked to contrasting attributes and actions. The most prevalent indication of imbalance lies in the deficiency of focusing on a single task, however, individuals lacking creativity or with an impaired memory may also exhibit a dearth of energy in the sixth chakra. Indications of a considerable discrepancy encompass the presence of persistent nocturnal visions, perceptual distortions, irrational beliefs, or an unwarranted sense of extreme suspicion.

The sixth chakra governs cognitive functioning and the central nervous system. The visual organs, auditory organs, olfactory organ, as well as the endocrine glands, are all intricately linked to this central source of energy. Any deviations present in this context could potentially indicate an asymmetry. Ocular fatigue, auditory impairments, cephalalgia, vertigo, or spinal ailments are indicative of a minor disparity; whereas migraines, neurologic impairment, cerebrovascular accident, convulsions, hemorrhage, or neoplasms may suggest a significantly greater discrepancy.

METHODS FOR ALIGNING THE THIRD EYE CHAKRA

Spend time in nature. Engage in avian observation or embark on a visit to an aquatic life exhibit. Exhibit preferred artistic creations, floral arrangements, and photographic masterpieces within the confines of your abode. Engage in a visitation to an art gallery. Refrain from frowning and instead exhibit a pleasant expression when gazing upon your reflection in the looking glass. Use positive affirmations. Visualize success. Develop a novel culinary creation. Enroll in a course focused on the artistic mediums of clay sculpting or woodworking. Play memory games. Practice dream recall. Redecorate. Engage in activities such as coloring, sketching, painting, capturing images through photography, or creating a scrapbook. Pursue an exploration of the esoteric sciences, encompassing divinatory practices such as tarot reading, oracle cards, runes, as well as the study of astrology. Use visual meditation. Kindly explore the subsequent yoga postures: kneeling, lotus, sage.

THE CROWN

Topmost part of Head – Ivory – Intellect

An equilibrium of the crown chakra can potentially foster a profound spiritual alignment with the universal energetic essence. It has the potential to bestow wisdom and mastery upon an individual's life. Alternatively, it can manifest itself through various subtle means, such as an egocentric deed, a meticulously reasoned choice, inquiries posed with genuine curiosity, or a gesture of compassion.

An imbalance in the crown chakra engenders cognitive perplexity. It arises from a dearth of trust, constrained convictions, and skepticism towards matters of spirituality. An individual could potentially lack direction, experience feelings of melancholy, display indifference, prioritize material possessions, or exhibit a sense of disconnect from existence.

The seventh chakra, serving as the final energy center, assumes the responsibility of regulating the body's response to physical stimuli. It regulates the functions of the brain stem, spinal cord, nervous system, pineal gland, muscular and skeletal systems, as well as the integumentary system. Any irregularities observed within these regions may indicate the existence of a sealed gateway. Exhibiting heightened sensitivity to light or sound, particularly to an excessive degree, signifies the presence of a barrier or impediment. Chronic fatigue, recurring headaches, degenerative ailments, a brain neoplasm, memory loss, or cognitive impairments are additional indicators of the blockage of the passageway.

What is Meditation?

The act of directing one's attention and engaging in profound contemplation, popularly known as meditation, possesses a long-standing heritage traceable to ancient civilizations and is embraced by diverse cultural and religious affiliations across the globe. The most ancient indication that we possess regarding the existence of meditation is derived from the depiction of wall arts found in the Indus Valley, which are believed to have originated between 5,000 and 3,500 BCE. The depicted individuals are shown in a position commonly associated with meditation, wherein they are sitting on the ground with their hands resting on their knees and their legs crossed. This posture is widely acknowledged as the preeminent stance of meditative practice.

The ancient scriptures of India have provided us with meditation techniques dating back more than 3,000 years. In contemporary times, meditation has transcended its traditional religious connotations and has come to be predominantly employed as a prevailing technique to cultivate tranquility of the mind and elicit sensations of serenity and rejuvenation. Due to the diverse nature of its practice, meditation encompasses numerous variations. For those who are new to this practice and seek to derive its benefits, presented below is a compilation of the predominant types of meditation.

Transcendental Meditation, a simplified technique of meditation, involves the repetition of a personally designated mantra—an often recognized and soothing word or phrase—in a specific manner.

Mindfulness Meditation: It entails achieving a state of complete presence and mental coherence, wherein one attains harmony with their thoughts while disregarding external distractions.

Mantra Meditation: This particular meditation approach involves the utilization of a mantra, which refers to a soothing word or phrase, for the purpose of preventing the individual from being interrupted by distracting thoughts during the meditative practice.

Vipassana Meditation, originating from ancient India, is a profound form of introspection that allows one to perceive reality in its unadulterated state, aligning with the essence of the Sanskrit term Vipassana.

Mindful Visualization: This is an approach whereby one engages in the visualization of serene mental imagery or scenarios.

Loving-Kindness Meditation, also referred to as Metta meditation, involves the deliberate expression of benevolent intentions towards others.

Yoga Meditation, an age-old Indian tradition, entails the execution of various body postures combined with controlled breathing techniques. Its objective lies in cultivating mental tranquility and enhancing physical flexibility.

Chakra Meditation: This practice encompasses a series of intentional exercises aimed at promoting relaxation, rejuvenation, and the harmonization of your chakras, thereby fostering spiritual vitality within your being.

The practice of meditation carries great significance for individuals seeking to attain equilibrium and restore harmony to their chakras. However, could you kindly explain the mechanics behind the efficacy of chakra meditation? The cosmos that envelops us bestows its celestial vitality upon the Earth and our bodily organs and glands, which are dispersed within our circulatory system and corporeal structure. This life force energy is essential not only to maintain but gain our optimum health and wellbeing. Given the interconnectedness and mutual influence of the chakras, engaging in meditative practices and harnessing this divine energy can enable us to attain an optimal state of equilibrium.

In order to initiate your journey into the transformative practice of chakra meditation, it is advisable to initially assume a seated position that induces a sense of ease and comfort, while ensuring that your spinal alignment remains upright but relaxed. Afterwards, direct your attention to each individual region of your physique that aligns with the respective positions of the seven chakras, commencing with your lower extremities and progressing upwards. Remain in each portion until a sense of relaxation is attained, as the stress dissipates.

Subsequently, it is advisable to direct your attention towards your breathing. Please refrain from exerting pressure on your breath, and instead allow it to naturally deepen and stabilize. As one experiences the tendency of the mind to drift (which is particularly common among novices), it is advisable to redirect one's attention to the breath and steadfastly maintain focus on each exhalation and inhalation. When your attention is fully concentrated, envisage the inhalation of oxygen into your respiratory system, followed by its progression into your circulatory system. Observe how it sustains and provides nourishment to all the vital components within your body, including organs, cells, and muscles, while simultaneously eliminating toxins that are expelled through each exhaled breath.

During your chakra meditation, you will subsequently visualize the pulsation of your heart and the seamless functionality of your physical body. You will witness the seamless collaboration among different components of your physique, working in unison to achieve perfect harmony. The respiration process sustains every aspect of the human anatomy, as the collective components coalesce to form the entirety of the physical frame. The breath serves as the vital energy that circulates and energizes the entire physiological system.

Subsequently, the vitality that sustains your physical being is intricately linked to the surrounding atmosphere, resulting in an emanation of energy that manifests as a hue resembling a shade of yellowish-orange. This energy shall envelop your entire being and permeate your aura. As this vibrant energy permeates your aura, you will witness its amplification and luminosity, imbued with profound vitality. Please remember to approach this location gradually, one step at a time. Sustain the momentum of your energy with every inhalation and allow your aura to further enhance its radiance.

At present, it is an opportune moment to activate and enhance the energy flow in all of your chakras, commencing with the aforementioned position of the root chakra. Envision a clockwise circulation of energy whereby the vitality present in your breath nourishes the spiraling motion, progressively intensifying its luminosity and potency. This vital energy revitalizes and harmonizes the foundational energy center within your being.

After ensuring the proper alignment of your root chakra, the next step entails progressing towards the sacral chakra. In a similar vein, it is imperative to adhere to the identical procedure here, just as one would with the solar plexus chakra, the heart chakra, the throat chakra, the third eye chakra, and ultimately, the crown chakra. Every individual will receive an infusion of vitality to restore equilibrium. Please refrain from concerning yourself with the specific duration you ought to spend at each given location. Devote an ample amount of time towards experiencing, with utmost attention, the purging, invigorating, and tranquilizing of each bodily region that aligns with its respective chakra.

It is imperative that one does not bypass a chakra, as they are intricately interconnected and mutually exert influence upon each other. Therefore, it would be prudent to begin at the base and ascend systematically, harmonizing each chakra before proceeding, in order to prevent any potential negative consequences from manifesting throughout the entirety of the process. The final stage of chakra meditation involves visualizing the simultaneous energization of all your chakras, accompanied by the clarity, radiance, and heightened vitality of your aura resulting from this vital life force.

Ultimately, it is advisable to gently open your eyes and maintain your position to allow for a brief period of relaxation, ensuring that your eyes remain open. Please exercise caution when focusing on the sensations and vitality of your rejuvenated physical state. It is crucial to exert diligent effort towards your meditation practice, with unwavering focus on each individual chakra, as they collectively constitute an interconnected system. In order for the system to achieve equilibrium, it is imperative to consider and contemplate all its components rather than solely focusing on one aspect, as that alone cannot guarantee resolution of the problem at hand.

As your level of expertise increases, you will develop an enhanced ability to discern and address discrete obstructions, thereby effectively channeling your meditative concentration towards specific chakras. It is important to consider that in order to engage in this activity, an estimated duration of one hour, perhaps slightly longer, may be required. Therefore, if you are pressed for time, it is advisable to select an appropriate moment as each chakra requires a considerable amount of time for adequate treatment and invigoration.

Nonetheless, meditation serves a broader purpose beyond the attainment of chakra equilibrium. It possesses numerous advantages that are widely acknowledged, even by the scientific community. As an example, consistent engagement in meditation will yield a discernible decrease in stress levels, a primary motivation for many individuals to embark on a meditative practice. Typically, the presence of both physical and mental stress typically results in elevated cortisol levels, which is the hormone associated with stress. Consequently, this hormone precipitates a plethora of deleterious consequences associated with stress, including sleep disturbance, heightened anxiety, despondency, elevated blood pressure, and exhaustion.

Meditation can support individuals in managing anxiety, as it fosters a reduction in stress levels, thereby contributing to a decrease in anxiety. Furthermore, it aids in mitigating the symptoms associated with a range of anxiety disorders, including but not limited to social anxiety, phobias, paranoid ideation, panic episodes, and obsessive-compulsive tendencies. Additionally, the attainment of an optimal state of emotional well-being can be facilitated through various meditation practices, which have the potential to engender a heightened sense of positivity towards existence and an enhanced level of self-assurance and self-perception. Mindfulness meditation is frequently advised for individuals seeking to cultivate and preserve their emotional well-being.

Increased self-awareness is an additional advantage that can be derived from regular meditation practice, as it facilitates a deeper understanding of oneself and fosters personal growth towards one's highest potential. As an example, the practice of self-inquiry meditation will not only foster enhanced self-awareness but also facilitate a deeper comprehension of one's interconnectedness with those in their immediate social sphere. There exist alternative methods of meditation that facilitate the identification and comprehension of one's self-defeating and harmful thoughts through an enhanced awareness of thought patterns. When confronted with negative thoughts, you will acquire the skill to redirect them towards more advantageous avenues.

Individuals who engage in the practice of focused-attention meditation have attested to a positive extension of their cognitive ability to sustain focus. This particular style of meditation enhances and fortifies your capacity to sustain attention, thus augmenting the endurance of your focal abilities. Engaging in brief sessions of meditation can prove highly advantageous in enhancing one's ability to sustain focus. As an illustration, it has been determined through a conclusive study that a mere duration of four days of engaging in such meditation practice proves to be sufficient.

Furthermore, it has been documented that meditation potentially mitigates age-related memory decline. As previously indicated, the practice of meditation enhances our cognitive acuity and focus, two elements that may assist in preserving youthful mental faculties, irrespective of chronological age. The practice of Kirtan Kriya involves the simultaneous utilization of vocalized chants or mantras and the repetitive movements of the fingers in order to concentrate and direct one's thoughts. Meditation has demonstrated considerable potential in partially ameliorating memory-related concerns, particularly in individuals afflicted with dementia.

Kindness can undoubtedly be cultivated through the practice of meditation, as various forms of meditation have been found to enhance benevolent behaviors towards others and oneself, in addition to fostering positive emotions. For instance, the meditation practice known as loving-kindness or Metta, as mentioned earlier, initiates by cultivating benevolent sentiments and thoughts towards oneself. As one continues to engage in regular practice, they acquire the ability to extend this virtue of forgiveness and benevolence not only to close companions, but also to acquaintances and eventually, to adversaries.

Meditation is a beneficial practice that is also advised for individuals experiencing addictive tendencies. This can be observed due to the fact that in order to fully engage in a meditation practice, one must cultivate their cognitive restraint. This cultivation, in turn, can facilitate the mitigation of dependencies by bolstering one's mindfulness and self-regulation abilities, ultimately leading to a deeper comprehension of the underlying catalysts for addictive behaviors. Based on empirical findings, scholarly studies indicate that meditation offers individuals the potential to acquire insight into redirecting their attention, enhancing self-control, comprehending the underlying factors of addictive tendencies, and managing impulses such as food cravings and emotional fluctuations.

Numerous individuals are afflicted, or will be afflicted, by insomnia at some juncture in their lifetimes. The practice of mindfulness meditation can facilitate the enhancement of sleep quality, as it effectively directs and redirects the excessive and intrusive thoughts that frequently trigger insomnia. It will facilitate tranquil relaxation of your body and induce a state of peacefulness by alleviating tension. Consequently, there is an increased probability that you will experience drowsiness and succumb to slumber. Likewise, the practice of meditation contributes to pain management, as our experience of pain is intricately tied to our mental state, which can be fortified during moments of stress. Through the practice of meditation, one will continue to encounter physical discomfort, yet gradually cultivate a heightened capacity to manage and perhaps even perceive a diminished sense of pain.

All of these meditation advantages are supported by scientific research and not only warrant investing your time in the practice of meditation, but should also serve as a compelling catalyst for initiating your meditation practice. Presented herewith are guidance and suggestions for engaging in a form of meditation distinct from chakra-focused meditation.

Guided Script For Practicing Sacral Chakra Meditation

The primary emphasis of this guided meditation lies in purifying the Sacral Chakra. This particular energy center is commonly referred to as Svadhishthana in the Sanskrit language, and its specific anatomical position is situated within the lower abdominal region, precisely posterior to the naval.

Please allocate a brief period of time to locate a suitable posture for meditation. In an ideal scenario, you are in a state of being seated in an upright posture. You have the option to either take a seat on the floor or on a chair.

Ensure that the thighs are positioned above the knees while sitting on the floor, as this will safeguard the knee joints against excessive rotational movements beyond their inherent range. Such movements have the potential to extend the ligaments and subsequently cause stretching. If required, please consider using a cushion or multiple cushions to heighten the hips while seated.

When assuming a seated position, it is important to ensure that both feet are able to comfortably rest upon the ground, while also ensuring that the back of the knees align with the edge of the chair.

Then, once you have established a stable stance, proceed to place your palms gently on the area of your lower abdomen.

Please take a few moments to engage in rhythmic respiration, allowing your breath to flow effortlessly and harmoniously. This will help cultivate a profound awareness of your physical presence and the present moment.

The sacral chakra is correlated with the hue of orange. Now, while maintaining one's hands gently placed on the lower abdomen, envision a vibrant orange glow emerging from the depths of the abdominal region. Behind the naval. A circle of orange.

This illumination evokes a sense of tranquility, serenity, and a gentle warmth.

Permit the illumination to persist while you remain in this location.

The body exhibits a stable condition. The breath is easy. The luminous orange light emits a comforting warmth.

The chakras serve as vortices of energy that facilitate the circulation of energy throughout the body. They rotate in order to facilitate the arrival and subsequent departure of energy, ensuring that the chakra-enhanced energy can be effectively directed to its requisite destination.

When an obstruction occurs within the sacral chakra, one can experience sensations of fatigue and heightened vulnerability, thereby increasing susceptibility to illnesses such as colds. Allergies have the potential to exert a more pronounced impact on your well-being, potentially leading to a diminished sexual desire.

A obstructed sacral chakra also exerts influence on one's mental state - leading to potential feelings of ennui, hypersensitivity, or lack of motivation. One might experience an immense feeling of guilt or exhibit apprehension towards alterations in their life. When there is an obstruction in the energetic flow of this chakra, it amplifies feelings of low self-esteem and envy.

On the other hand, in juxtaposition, when the sacral chakra experiences equilibrium, individuals may perceive a sense of assurance and possess a heightened perception of their own intrinsic value. It is relatively more effortless to forge genuine connections and engage in authentic interaction with women, thereby fostering an openness towards embracing change with enthusiasm and optimism, as opposed to succumbing to fear. You possess the capacity to release feelings of guilt and attain a heightened sense of emotional self-regulation. Moreover, you experience increased creativity and inspiration, along with improved abilities in problem-solving.

All of those outcomes are attainable for you.

Facilitating the purification and unobstructed movement of the sacral chakra will enhance one's perception and engagement with the joys of existence.

This is not only attainable for you, but you are actively engaged in its pursuit at present. By engaging in the practice of mentally picturing the orange line located in the lower abdominal area, you are effectively facilitating the unobstructed circulation of energy throughout the Svadhishthana chakra, thereby allowing it to disperse its dynamic, innovative, and assured energy throughout the entirety of your being.

Notice the orange glow.

It warms the abdomen.

And you maintain a gentle respiration while persistently observing it.

At present, the orange sphere initiates its rotational motion. Gradually, with an initially slow pace, and subsequently accelerating; accumulating energy along its path and transmitting energy outward, via the body's conduits of energy.

Initially, as the sphere rotates, it becomes apparent that one or two obsidian markers are present within it. These are blockages. It rotates, yet its movements are hindered; it appears to stumble upon these dark blemishes, restrained by their existence.

However, as the rotation persists, the black regions progressively diminish in size.

They decrease in size progressively.

The orange hue intensifies, projecting a more vivid and radiant appearance.

Upon the reduction of the black regions, there is a noticeable enhancement in the rotational movement of the orange sphere, designated as the Svadhishthana chakra. It gradually sheds its inhibitions, ceasing to stutter or halt amidst its rapid whirling.

The black spots gradually diminish in size until they ultimately vanish.

And subsequently, the sacral chakra rotates continuously. It exhibits a lack of restraint; it is evident.

It cyclically rotates, incessantly turns, and imparts warmth to the core of your being with its radiant illumination. As the rotation ensues, a surge of imaginative vigour courses through your being.

Allow yourself to calmly embrace this surge of authority. This energy has perennially resided within your being. You are establishing an environment in which it can effortlessly propagate.

Return to the revolving orange orb of the sacral chakra.

Consider a scenario in which the energy emanating from it exhibits undulating patterns akin to waves, permeating your physical form and expanding in all directions. As the ripple effect extends through the corporeal form, it likewise permeates the ethereal layers encompassing one's energetic state, cognitive faculties, and emotional disposition.

These undulations evoke within you a heightened sense of self-value. Your value. Your inherent fortitude, and the manifestation of radiance, affection, and magnificence that emanate from you.

These undulations instill within you a sense of assurance regarding your aptitude to effectively communicate and establish rapport with women. It is understood that one has the freedom to engage in interactions in a genuine and unrestricted manner, being true to oneself. There are no impediments that would prevent you from establishing profound and enriching relationships with others.

These undulations evoke a sense of exhilaration towards the prospects that lie ahead. We extend a warm welcome to all that lies ahead. You eagerly anticipate the impending transformations in your life, as you possess the creative aptitude and self-assurance required to navigate any challenge. Nothing is too much. You exhibit autonomy and possess a heightened awareness of your own capacities.

Absorb this knowledge.

"Inhale the hue of orange."

Inhale assurance.

Now, softly return your focus to your breath.

Do not attempt to exert control over it. Merely observe its inherent cadence.

The sensation of cold air permeating the nostrils upon inhalation, juxtaposed with the expulsion of warm air during exhalation.

Gaining consciousness of the inhalation and exhalation.

And as one attains mindfulness of their breath, they regain a sense of spatial awareness. Sitting in this place. Calmly being here. You possess cognizance of your immediate surroundings - the encompassing environment that shall unveil before your eyes upon awakening, within a brief span of time.

Extend the arms upwards, separating them from the lower abdomen, and converge the palms, uniting them in front of the chest.

With the subsequent inhalation, elevate the arms upward, extending them over the head. To the highest extent possible while keeping the palms joined together.

Next, proceed to release a deep breath while gracefully lowering the arms in a controlled manner on both sides of your body, allowing the shoulders to fully unwind in the process. With the following inhalation, reunite the palms in a gesture of togetherness before the sternum once more. Inhale deeply and exhale audibly through the nostrils.

Ultimately, position the palms of the hands over the eyes. Gently close your eyes for a brief period, allowing them to acclimate to the brightness that lies ahead after being in the darkness. And subsequently, remove your hands at a pace that suits you.

Your practice has been successfully accomplished.

Meditations For The Solar Plexus Chakra

The solar plexus chakra represents your third energetic center and is alternatively referred to as Manipura, a Sanskrit term that translates to "brilliant jewel" or "radiant gem." This particular chakra is situated in the area above your abdominal region, concurrently below the lower boundary of your rib cage. The solar plexus represents your intuitive faculty, which can also be referred to as your instinctual response or commonly known as your 'gut' feeling. This particular chakra symbolizes an individual's determination, self-concept, assurance, and sagacity. This is where your self-esteem and self-discipline are located. It facilitates the harnessing of one's volition to attain aspirations and ambitions; thus, translating mere verbal expressions and contemplation into tangible deeds. The color yellow is symbolized as a representation of cheerfulness, energy, encouragement, joy, and intellect.

When in equilibrium, you experience a sense of empowered determination that enables you to effectively achieve any goal you devote yourself to. You possess abundant vitality and exuberance that enable you to enthusiastically engage in your daily pursuits. You possess the capacity to confront and overcome the various challenges and adversities that arise in your life. You possess a strong sense of self-assurance and exhibit elevated levels of self-worth. Nevertheless, when there is an imbalance in the solar plexus, individuals often experience a sense of powerlessness in the face of specific circumstances within their lives. They consistently strive to remain in command of every situation, and upon realizing their inability to do so, they tend to exhibit reactionary behavior characterized by anger and frustration. Alternatively, individuals may begin to experience a diminished sense of purpose in their daily existence. Rather than embracing life's opportunities wholeheartedly, they may increasingly view it as burdensome, leading to a withdrawal from social interactions and a lack of drive. From a physiological standpoint, you may encounter issues pertaining to blood sugar, liver function, digestive disorders, hypertension, and persistent fatigue.

One can initiate the process of unblocking their chakras by incorporating yellow-hued edibles into their diet, such as bananas, grains, corn, yellow peppers, along with the inclusion of complex carbohydrates to ensure an ample supply of energy. Please ensure to limit the consumption of excessive sugary foods. The consumption of chamomile tea has been found to be effective in alleviating obstructions in the solar plexus region as well. Additionally, one can begin incorporating the color yellow into their wardrobe within the confines of their home, or enhance the aesthetic of their living space by adorning it with vibrant yellow-hued flowers.

Mindful meditation practice tailored to activate the energy center known as the solar plexus chakra.

Assume an upright and comfortable posture either on the floor or on a chair. Commence your meditation practice by inhaling and exhaling in a measured and profound manner. Please take the time required to unwind your body and muscles, as well as refocus your mind, so that you can gradually transition into the state of closing your eyes. One can achieve this by directing their attention towards and consciously relaxing various body areas, starting with the lower limbs, followed by the abdomen, chest, upper extremities, shoulders, neck, and finally, the head, progressively moving upwards along the body. One may also choose to shift their attention towards the expansiveness of their chest and body as they inhale, or the contraction of their chest and body as they exhale. By redirecting your attention away from your thoughts, you can effectively alleviate any concerns or troubles, thus fostering mental clarity.

While assuming a seated position, begin to establish a connection and perceive the temperature, whether cool or warm, emanating from the floor and the earth below. Envision the upward transmission of energy originating from the earth, coursing through your physical being. Direct your attention to the upward movement of this energy, as it traverses towards the area of the solar plexus situated amidst your abdominal area, specifically between the navel and the lower edge of your rib cage.

Envision a golden radiance materializing and extending within that vicinity, steadily revolving in a clockwise direction and progressively growing with each inhalation. Experience the comforting warmth and sensory stimulation emitted by the yellow light, evoking deeply-felt emotional responses. Dwell in that sensation momentarily prior to unveiling your eyes for a brief respite, subsequently progressing with your day.

If it is within your capacity to venture outdoors during conditions of sunshine and warmth, it is recommended that you avail yourself of the opportunity. Please position yourself either standing or seated in a location where you are exposed to direct sunlight. Proceed by gently closing your eyes. Direct your attention towards the area of your body that experiences the most warmth due to solar radiation. Experience and acknowledge the comforting heat bestowed upon you, whilst embracing the delightful tingling sensations permeating your entire being. Subsequently, begin to direct your focus towards your inner self. Please observe the sensation of the ground beneath you; does it feel cold or warm? Are you experiencing any sensations of tingling or pulsations in that area? What is your view regarding the area that is situated above your head? Does it give the sensation of a vast cosmos looming overhead, exerting a gentle force upon your cranium?

Extend your arms upwards unimpeded, directing your focus towards the celestial expanse above, while taking a deep breath and perceiving the ethereal realm enveloping you. Imagine a radiant golden flame emanating from the tips of your fingers, experiencing its connection as it courses through your hands and descends towards the upper abdominal region, precisely the area where the solar plexus is situated. Exhale and gradually lower your arms towards the ground. Please lower your hands to the ground and experience the soil underneath, along with the harmonious equilibrium of vitality and vitality adjoining you.

Take another breath in, while simultaneously extending your hands upwards, illustrating the act of harmonizing your energy with the radiant sun above. Allow the radiant yellow light to flow downwards, reaching your solar plexus region, purifying and unlocking the energy center located therein. Please take note of your current emotional state: do you experience feelings of tranquility, equilibrium, and contentment? Reiterate the manual gestures for a duration of a few minutes or at your discretion. To conclude, return your hands to their original position on the ground. Take a moment to inhale deeply while maintaining an open mindset for a duration of one minute before allowing your eyes to open. Survey your surroundings and direct your gaze towards the expanse of the sky or the terrain beneath your feet, immersing yourself in the present moment for a brief interval, relishing the natural environment surrounding you, prior to proceeding with your daily activities.

To restore equilibrium to this chakra, it is imperative to cultivate a capacity for embracing love and compassion within one's heart. Avoid harboring resentments, rather cultivate the virtue of forgiveness and progress forward. One may choose to offer prayers to the universe, beseeching it to transmit one's sentiments of affection to those in one's vicinity. Upon achieving a greater capacity for empathy and fostering a culture of benevolence, the benevolence one exhibits towards others will inevitably reciprocate.

Restoring balance to this chakra necessitates a considerable amount of determination, as you must conquer your shyness and venture beyond your comfort zone to attain triumph. Proceed gradually and incrementally. A pertinent concept that can be applied in this scenario is known as 'simulate success until it is attained.' This principle entails assuming the appearance and behaviors associated with the desired outcome until the desired outcome is ultimately achieved. If your desire is to exude confidence, then embody confidence through your actions. Additionally, you may consider incorporating positive affirmations:"

I possess an attractive appearance and exude self-assurance."

I possess the capability to succeed in any endeavor that I choose to devote my mental faculties towards."

I am encouraged to actively pursue my aspirations."

I possess remarkable strength and resilience."

I am liberating myself from detrimental past encounters."

When one undergoes the process of opening this particular chakra, there is a possibility of encountering the re-emergence of past apprehensions. This occurrence arises as a result of the body and mind endeavoring to release these fears, thereby purifying the individual's physical being. You may exhibit unprovoked aggression, experiencing feelings of resentment towards individuals whom you would refrain from vocally expressing your dissatisfaction towards. You may experience a sensation of nausea in your body, potentially leading to vomiting in certain instances. Nevertheless, you will undoubtedly express gratitude towards yourself for attaining the proficiency to unlock this chakra as it serves as the fundamental tool in propelling you towards triumph and actualizing your aspirations. It imparts the necessary drive and resolve to excel in any endeavor you choose to pursue.

Incorporating Stones For The Alignment Of Your Chakras

The notion of utilizing crystals or gemstones to align your chakras is based on the premise that each of these stones possesses the ability to harmonize or enhance the specific energy centers you concentrate on. When making a selection of stones to engage with, it is advisable to take into account the various attributes possessed by each stone. These attributes may include factors such as the stone's color, the quality of its energy, and any personal inclination you may experience towards the stone.

Choosing the Appropriate Crystal or Stone for Therapeutic Purposes:

To effectively select the suitable stone for the purpose of aligning and harmonizing your chakras, it is imperative to acquire knowledge regarding the specific stones associated with each individual chakra. Please be aware that every chakra may correspond to numerous crystals, and engaging in exploration and experimentation with various varieties can assist you in selecting the most suitable option.

Exploring Various Alternatives: It is worth noting that certain gemstones, corresponding to distinct chakras, may exhibit efficacy in addressing particular ailments, while other gemstones may be effective in treating remaining conditions. It is possible that one stone may prove suitable to you temporarily, only to lose its appeal as another one beckons for your attention. In my observation, I have come to the conclusion that durations of approximately one month at maximum yield optimal outcomes in the realm of stone healing.

Taking into consideration Intuition: It is crucial to acknowledge that intuition holds significant influence in the process of chakra healing. Utilize your discernment to select an appropriate stone for the purpose of healing or restoring equilibrium to your chakra systems. To accomplish this, utilize your heightened faculty of intuition. This could encompass the identification of crystals and determining which one exudes the greatest luminosity to individuals. This could also encompass attempting to sense the stone's energy through manual contact. One may also discern the correct choice through visual inspection.

Crystals Suitable for Balancing the Chakras:

Every individual chakra within your energy system typically corresponds with a specific selection of gemstones. Once you have identified the specific chakra or chakras in need of healing, you can select the appropriate crystal or stone for that purpose. The majority of these stones are available for purchase through online platforms or from specialized establishments that cater to the new age or crystal niche. Following is an assortment of items to initiate your endeavor:

The crimson-hued, foundational Chakra: Crystals pertinent to this vital energy hub encompass black tourmaline, tiger's eye, bloodstone, fire agate, and hematite. Additionally, one may opt for crimson-hued stones of a more generic nature.

The Orange Chakra, specifically located in the Sacral region of the body, can be harmonized and balanced through the utilization of various gemstones such as coral, moonstone, carnelian, and citrine. Additionally, you have the option to select crystals or stones of a general nature that exhibit an orange color.

The Solar Plexus Chakra, which is colored in a vibrant shade of yellow, offers a variety of gemstones to choose from. Among them are topaz, citrine, calcite, and the esteemed malachite.

The Heart Chakra in Green Hue: Gemstones suitable for harmonizing the heart chakra energy center encompass green tourmaline, green calcite, jade, or rose quartz.

The Blue Throat Chakra: To harmonize your throat chakra, opt for blue gemstones such as aquamarine, turquoise, or lapis lazuli.

The Violet Ajna Chakra: When it comes to your ajna chakra, you have the option of choosing either obsidian or amethyst.

The White, Crown Chakra: To restore equilibrium in this chakra, it is advisable to opt for gemstones like diamond, amethyst, quartz, or selenite.

In addition to utilizing stones or crystals for the purpose of chakra healing, it is also feasible to incorporate the hue affiliated with the specific chakra requiring alignment by adorning oneself or immersing oneself in such color. Furthermore, the act of envisioning the hue continuously during the course of the day can provide assistance.

The Mechanism of Action of these Therapeutic Crystals:

Stones exhibit the capacity to activate, enhance, or harmonize the chakra energy systems within your body. Healing through the utilization of crystals is predicated on the notion that these crystalline entities possess inherent vibrational frequencies that can be harnessed to promote healing, by harmonizing the flow of energy within the chakra system. In terms of these stones, each exhibits a distinct vibrational signature, and each stone aligns or corresponds with specific chakras or energetic centers within your physical and spiritual being.

Enabling: You have the ability to activate this healing power by relying on your own intuition or intention. Engaging in visual exercises or employing the power of imagination can be instrumental in cultivating a mindset that enables you to optimize your experiences. Make an effort to attain a mental state that facilitates the integration of the stones with complementary techniques aimed at balancing your chakras.

Facilitation: These stones facilitate the amplification and directed flow of vibrations and energy, allowing them to interact with the frequencies and vibrations of the targeted chakra upon which you focus your attention during the exercise.

Adorning oneself with Chakra Crystals:

You may also consider incorporating these crystals or stones into your jewelry selections. Make an effort to select a crystal or stone that aligns harmoniously with your individual energy or corresponds to the chakra that requires attention or alignment. Every crystal is accompanied by its own distinct therapeutic properties, spiritual objectives, and emotional reflections. Additionally, you may be inclined towards a particular color on a given day. Please be advised that the potency of this stone intensifies as your objectives become more defined, therefore exercise caution when choosing your preferred options. By adorning oneself with stones or crystals to symbolize the chakras and facilitate their healing, one demonstrates a testament not only to oneself but also to others. These naturally occurring elements of the earth possess considerable efficacy in the attraction of specific energies towards oneself or the amplification of pre-existing ones. They may also harbor divergent connotations contingent upon cultural contexts.

A Guide on the Application of Crystals and Stones for Balancing your Chakras:

Numerous techniques are available to harness the potential of these stones to promote personal well-being and restoration. Once you have chosen the stone that you wish to utilize:

Position it: Situate it in proximity to the area of the chakra in need of harmonization. This task can be easily accomplished when in a supine position, but it is equally feasible to execute it while seated or upright. Provided that the stone remains in close proximity, it will function effectively.

Direct your attention: Presently, you have the ability to activate the stone by directing your focus towards the specific chakra that requires assistance, employing either meditation or intention. Furthermore, apart from these aforementioned practices, one can also direct their attention towards harnessing the therapeutic attributes of the stone by tapping into their intuitive faculties.

Revitalizing or Purifying the Stones: It is crucial to revitalize and purify the crystals or stones before and after their usage. This can be achieved through the exposition of the objects to either sunlight or moonlight for a duration of 24 hours. Additionally, it is possible to immerse them in a receptacle containing fresh water derived from a natural source, such as the ocean or a river.

"Comprehensive Color-Based Therapy for Chakra Equilibrium:

When acquiring the knowledge of self-healing through the utilization of colors, it is important to bear in mind that the chakras exhibit the presence of intersecting hues within them. To grasp this concept, consider the manner in which different hues of paint blend harmoniously. You commence with primary colors such as yellow, red, and blue, progressing towards secondary colors such as purple, green, or orange.

Options for Stones or Color Combinations: These secondary colors will serve to enhance the primary colors that arise through the amalgamation of two primary colors. This suggests that the combination of a red stone and a blue stone can be employed to restore balance to your crown chakra, which is associated with the color purple.

Maintaining Equilibrium: It is essential to bear in mind that while focusing on the restoration of a particular chakra, one must ensure harmonious stability by attending to the hue that is inversely aligned. As an illustration, when undertaking the healing process for your green heart chakra, it is advisable to enhance this endeavor by directing your attention towards the red root chakra as well.

Engaging in this practice will aid in the preservation of the equilibrium within your complete chakra network, guaranteeing harmonious alignment and the attainment of their utmost potential.

CHAPTER THREE

Strategies for Activating the Chakras

One can achieve the activation of Chakras by means of engaging in meditative practices that include the utilization of specific sounds and mudras, which are intricate hand positions or gestures aimed at opening the Chakras. Mudras possess the capability to channel additional energy towards specific chakras, thereby augmenting the impact of the uttered sounds. Mudras are employed in the practice of yoga with the objective of cultivating an enhanced state of awareness towards the specific energetic realms encompassed within the subtle body.

OPENING MULADHARA

Muladhara serves as the pivotal groundwork for the remaining chakras, with its focal point residing at the midpoint between the genital region and the anus. Invert this mudra by reversing its orientation and gradually bringing down the arms to a certain extent, ensuring that the middle fingers are directed downwards towards the pelvic region, while simultaneously vocalizing the sonorous syllable "LAM."

OPENING SVADHISTHANA

Svadhisthana, also referred to as the sacral chakra, is associated with the feminine mudra, which serves to establish a connection between sensuality and sexuality. The mudra utilized is identified as Shakti. Direct your attention to the sacral chakra located in the lumbar region of your back. Place your hands in a clasping position on your lap, with the left hand positioned under the right hand, ensuring that the palm of the left hand touches the back of the right hand's fingers. Gently touch the tips of your thumbs together, and proceed to vocalize the sound "VAM" in a rhythmic repetition.

OPENING MANIPURA

This particular chakra utilizes the Rudra mudra, which facilitates the manifestation of the divine energy inherent in all yogic deities. Direct your attention to the navel chakra, positioning your hand in front of your finger slightly below the solar plexus with the fingers interlaced and pointing away from the body. It is imperative to ensure the extension of the fingers and interlocking of the thumbs. Additionally, vocalize the syllable RAM.

OPENING ANAHATA

This particular chakra utilizes the Padma mudra, drawing inspiration from the lotus flower, and facilitates the manifestation of affection and the invocation of novel opportunities. Direct your attention to the heart chakra located along the spine, aligned with the heart area. To initiate the opening gesture, connect the outer margins of your thumbs and pinky fingers, extend the fingertips, and maintain the palmar alignment by joining the base of your palms. The vocalization required for the activation of this particular chakra is the sound "YAM."

OPENING VISHUDDHA

This specific chakra has the ability to be activated through the utilization of the "Granthita" mudra, which can be applied around the throat area to assist in facilitating the process of articulating one's true and genuine identity. Direct your attention towards the throat chakra while positioning your fingers inwards, except for the thumb, and apply gentle upward pressure. This vocalization associated with the chakra is designated as HAM.

OPENING AJNA

This chakra is associated with the acquisition of profound understanding. To activate this chakra, position your hand just below the chest region, with the middle finger extended and pointing forward, the tips of the fingers should be in contact. It is advisable that one positions their thumbs towards oneself and brings them together at their tips while reciting the sound OM or AUM.

OPENING SAHASRARA

The chakra in question can be activated by employing the "mudra of a thousand petals", rendering it the utmost spiritual chakra. To activate the crown chakra, direct your attention towards the chakra situated at the apex of your head. Position your hands in front of your abdomen, with the ring finger of each hand pointing upwards and gently touching at their tips. Then, interlace the remaining fingers of your right hand over the left, ensuring that the left thumb rests beneath the right thumb. Proceed with repeating the resonant sound "NG" as you perform this practice.

Chakras, Contemplation, And Optimistic Declarations

To ensure the efficacy of your chakra healing meditation, it is imperative that you commit to memory the hues linked with each energy center. An appealing aspect lies in the fact that the process of meditation is not inflexible. You have the flexibility to engage in this activity in any location of your choosing, with the sole condition being that it is devoid of any audible disturbance. Moreover, it can be conveniently pursued whether you are in motion, at rest, or in a reclining position. The objective is to establish a connection not only with your individual identity but also with the transcendental plane to which you are inherently connected. Regardless of whether you possess a mere half-hour, quarter-hour, or even five minutes, the practice of meditative visualization remains attainable whenever you detect a state of physical or emotional disharmony.

1. Make a deliberate choice regarding the type of meditation you intend to engage in, and carefully create an appropriate environment. Will you lie down? Sit, or walk? Make appropriate adjustments to the temperature and lighting, and additionally, ensure the necessary oil blend is prepared for the designated energy center. Apply the blend onto the designated chakra region for the purpose of healing. As previously stated, a range of 1-3 drops typically suffices.

2. Please ensure that you designate a definitive time period for your meditation practice. Please power down your electronic devices and kindly inform your family or friends that you require a brief period of uninterrupted solitude.

3. Please take up the desired position. For individuals who are in a seated position, it is advisable to maintain proper posture by ensuring a straight

but relaxed alignment of the back. It is imperative that your feet make contact with the floor, serving as a means of grounding oneself. Reclining is advisable for shorter meditation sessions due to the propensity to drift into slumber. It is recommended that individuals who struggle to unwind unless they are in motion consider engaging in walking meditation. You have the option to navigate in circular patterns or proceed directly along a linear path.

4. Engage in mindful breathing practices while remaining attentive to your breath. It is commonly advised to engage in three full inhalations and exhalations for optimal benefit. Nevertheless, additional measures may be required, contingent upon the extent of your stress.

5. After achieving a state of relaxation, initiate the process of visualizing a sphere of radiant light. The hue of the luminous orb ought to align with the

chakra necessitating restoration. Direct your attention to the ball with utmost concentration, maintaining your focus for as long as possible. In the event that thoughts arise, acknowledge them without attachment, and swiftly redirect your attention to your breathing. Feel free to engage in this activity for any duration you desire. Your intuition will guide you in determining the appropriate moment to cease. Upon completion, release, unwind, and allow yourself to take a few additional deep breaths.

Please be aware that an alternative method is available whereby one can engage in a meditation practice that possesses the capability to restore balance and healing to all of the chakras simultaneously. Rather than visualizing a sphere of light, consider envisioning yourself ascending an escalator, with each chakra color perfectly aligned. The root chakra should be positioned at the lowest step, while the crown chakra color resides at the very top. Once you have reached the summit, cast your gaze downwards and behold a harmonious arrangement of vibrant hues.

Constructive and Restorative Affirmations for Individual Chakras

Positive and Healing Affirmations denote uplifting declarations that can be vocalized during moments of distress or when seeking to enhance one's attitude. These affirmations can be utilized at any time throughout the day. Despite the seemingly straightforward nature of the process, they have demonstrated significant effectiveness according to numerous studies, all of which have yielded positive outcomes.

Root Chakra

I am safe. I am loved.
I am entitled to be present in this setting.

I hold a strong conviction in the inherent rhythm of existence.

I have formed a deep connection with the natural world.

Sacral Chakra

I choose to associate myself with individuals who exude affection and compassion.

I am receptive to experiencing pleasure effortlessly.

I bring satisfaction to others.

I am deserving of physical enjoyment and satisfaction.

I possess a splendid physical and mental constitution.

I acknowledge and hold in high regard my cognitive and physical well-being.

Sexuality is an inherent facet of human nature and holds a profound level of sanctity.

Solar Plexus Chakra

I have a purpose.

I can guide myself.

My aspirations come to fruition on a daily basis.

I have garnered numerous accomplishments, of which I hold great pride.

I possess a natural aptitude for making decisions.

I am strong.

I am courageous.

I can do it.

Heart Chakra

I express empathy towards both myself and others.

Affection is endemic in our existence.

I am receptive to the experience of love, as it manifests as a profoundly exquisite emotion.

I forgive myself.

I possess the strength to extend forgiveness to others.

I express my gratitude for the opportunities presented by challenges. They shape me.

I possess the capability to foster the development of my inner child.

Throat Chakra

My preferred mode of communication entails transparency, integrity, and forthrightness.

I possess the ability to express my emotions effortlessly.

I am entitled to express my genuine thoughts and opinions.

I possess the ability to effectively communicate my creativity.

Communication allows for the dissemination of my experiences and knowledge.

Third Eye Chakra

I place my confidence in my innate intuition.

I trust my intuition.

I nurture my spirit.

I acknowledge and grant forgiveness to my previous actions and experiences.

I am receptive to the insights and knowledge bestowed upon me by the cosmic forces.

My life is precious.

Crown Chakra

I belong to the influential realm of spirituality.

While my life experiences may not be devoid of imperfection, I acknowledge and embrace them as an integral part of my journey.

I represent a manifestation of the cosmos.

Every day, I strive to embrace and fully inhabit the present moment.

I strongly encourage you to recite these affirmations on a daily basis, both in the morning and in the evening. Utter them with unwavering conviction and in a tone exuding affection. In the near future, you will undergo the experience of positive transformations.

The Throat Chakra

The pharynx serves as a conduit connecting the cranial region with the remainder of the bodily system. The significance of it cannot be exaggerated, which is why it is considered one of the seven primary energy centers in the human body. We employ our vocal apparatus situated in our throat to emanate sound waves in order to facilitate effective comprehension by others.

This particular Chakra symbolizes the convergence of various energies that harmoniously facilitate the process of communication. The verbal exchange constitutes merely a portion of the communications, as non-verbal cues such as body language, facial expressions, and emotional states play a crucial role. Individuals lacking the capacity to regulate their speech and emotions may inevitably utter remarks that have the potential to inflict harm upon both themselves and others. The use of emotive language carries a dual impact, similar to a double-edged blade, comprising both advantages and disadvantages. Consequently, one must possess the skill to wield it effectively. Individuals with a diminished vitality in their Throat Chakra may encounter challenges in employing appropriate verbal expression or articulation essential for effective interpersonal communication. These individuals possess a notable deficiency in articulating their thoughts proficiently, rendering their participation in conversations or discussions a formidable challenge.

The throat facilitates the production of vocal sound by enabling the functioning of the vocal cords. Vocalization occurs when we exhale air from our lungs and subsequently generate vibrations within the vocal box or vocal cords, enabling the production of speech. In circumstances where we experience negativity, it is customary for us to refrain from taking deep inhalations. In contrast, we engage in shallow respiration, leading to the accumulation of a higher concentration of harmful air particles within the respiratory system. The presence of additional impurity may give rise to deficiencies in communication and the emergence of complications. Hence, it is strongly advised to engage in the practice of deep breathing during moments of distress, as it facilitates the elimination of contaminants from both our respiratory system and our cognitive realms.

It is of utmost significance to enhance the Throat Chakra as it entails enhancing communication capabilities, articulate expression, and the ability to convey veracity. Achieving equilibrium of the Throat Chakra entails maintaining proficient and effective communication. There is no matter pertaining to voicing one's thoughts, articulating oneself without constraint, in a clear and authentic manner. The larynx serves as the anatomical location where vocalization can be produced. The manner in which you regulate your cognitive vitality within this Chakra is instrumental in effectively conveying your emotions and thoughts devoid of any impediments.

Conversely, the obstruction of the Throat Chakra may result in difficulties in the realm of communication. Frequently, it entails substantial disputes, miscommunication, and maintaining confidentiality. Furthermore, individuals often encounter instances where they are burdened with numerous thoughts yet struggle to articulate them effectively.

Thus, we should abandon feelings of anger, jealousy, hatred, and ego in order to achieve equilibrium within the Throat Chakra. Furthermore, the Throat Chakra encompasses not only verbal expression and communication, but also encompasses the capacity for attentive listening. Communication is a mutual exchange, as it were. This implies that proficiency in communication is not solely determined by one's speaking abilities, but also necessitates the skill of attentive listening.

Conversely, the hyperactive state of the Throat Chakra pertains to displaying excessive vocalization, audacity, strong opinions, engaging in gossip, or employing coarse and profane language.

Characteristics of the Throat Chakra"
"Overview of the Throat Chakra"
"Description of the Throat Chakra"
"Explanation of the Throat Chakra

Geographical Position: This particular Chakra can be found precisely at the midpoint of your neck, in close proximity to your throat.

Color Component: It is linked with the hue blue.

Sangkrit: It is referred to as Vishuddha in the Sangkrit language.

Fundament & Obligation: Communication serves as the primary fundament. This particular Chakra is renowned for its association with integrity, virtuous conduct, and the ability to create a favorable impression.

Yoga Asana and Chant: The designated yoga asana for the Throat Chakra entails performing the shoulder stand, a posture that involves elevating the throat region to facilitate the harmonious flow of emotional energies from the head to the rest of the body. The prescribed action entails intertwining your fingers and ensuring that both thumbs make contact with one another, subsequently positioning them near your abdomen. The recommended crystal for enhancing the energy of the Throat Chakra is the Labradorite crystal. In conjunction with the emanation of spearmint or peppermint scent, this Yoga practice will exclusively bestow upon you a sense of serenity.

Indicators for determining the state of your Throat Chakra's openness and balance include the ability to engage in effective and constructive communication and interaction with others. Furthermore, you possess qualities of integrity, empathy, and adeptness in active listening.

Next, we shall delineate the indications of a blockage or imbalanced state in your Throat Chakra. These encompass instances wherein you encounter a pervasive lack of understanding from others, readily make assumptions, or harbor undisclosed information due to a general lack of trust in others.

Indications of an excessively active Throat Chakra include the inclination to display disruptive behavior, expressing oneself in a snide and disagreeable manner when interacting with others. What is your basis for this knowledge? Several factors to be mindful of include your volume and demeanor, particularly avoiding the use of offensive language or profanity without just cause. Occasionally, individuals misconstrue the notion of truthfulness by displaying impolite behavior. They believe they are expressing the truth, but in reality, their insensitivity has a proclivity to cause harm to others. Additionally, engaging in idle chatter and displaying a tendency to interrupt others during discussions is indicative of an excessively stimulated Throat Chakra.

In order to enhance the condition of your Throat Chakra and ensure its well-being, it would be beneficial to engage in the practice of maintaining a journal or devising a To-do list. Engaging in the practice of expressing those aspects which are challenging to articulate, such as one's emotions and thoughts, can be regarded as a constructive approach to cultivating and enhancing the functionality of the Throat Chakra. It has become increasingly prevalent among contemporary youth to maintain a journal documenting the events of their daily lives. Such an activity serves not only as a catalyst for enhancing their creative abilities but also as a means to attain a state of optimal mental well-being. Additionally, venturing out and engaging with unfamiliar individuals can also enhance one's ability to communicate effectively and facilitate the development of proper conversational techniques.

The color Blue is attributed to the Throat Chakra. The azure hue of the celestial canopy, historically affirms the inherent connection between the color blue and the sky. In accordance with this phenomenon, it follows that the act of gazing upwards to behold the sky necessitates extending one's neck. Additionally, it is worth mentioning that the intake of fruits such as blueberries and purple sweet potatoes can provide essential nutrients that contribute to the harmonious functioning of your Throat chakra. Consuming a beverage consisting of the aforementioned constituents alongside a small portion of mint leaves will effectively enhance the vitality of the Throat Chakra.

The chakra associated with the sixth primary energy center

It appears insubstantial to note that we possess a quantity of eyes exceeding two. This phenomenon arises due to the fact that humans possess a mere pair of ocular organs. The concept of the third eye alludes to the internal reservoir of emotional prowess inherent within an individual. Both your ocular faculties play a crucial role in facilitating visual perception, however, your metaphysical perception, commonly referred to as the third eye, holds paramount significance in shaping your cognitive perspective, primarily pertaining to thoughts and introspection. The Third Eye Chakra symbolizes a juxtaposition of mental turbulence and serenity, encapsulating the experience of stress and persistent concerns that individuals struggle to overcome. Individuals sever their connection with the energies of this Chakra by means of emotional outbursts, illogical cognition, or involuntary physical actions.

The disruption of the Third Eye Chakra can precipitate enduring psychological conditions such as depression and anxiety. The Third Eye symbolizes the pineal gland. Although there exists a multitude of pseudoscientific literature on this particular anatomical feature, it does possess legitimate scientific applications that are directly relevant to this Chakra. As you may observe, this particular gland is responsible for the secretion of a hormone known as "melatonin." This hormone plays a crucial role in regulating our circadian rhythm and seasonal cycle. It informs us of the optimal times to rest and rise, determined by either natural light patterns or personal routines, without necessitating precise timekeeping.

Sleep facilitates the induction of an anabolic state that fosters growth, and plays a crucial role in the preservation of the overall health of our immune system, nervous system, skeletal system, and muscular system during the sleep cycle. In essence, slumber is imperative for the advancement of one's physical well-being and cognitive state. Individuals have a propensity to encounter suboptimal physical and cognitive growth in the event of irregular sleep patterns or inadequate sleep, whether attributable to occupational stress or any other causes. The Third Eye Chakra promotes relaxation by facilitating the generation of ample energy within the body during periods of rest and sleep. When an individual experiences a state of relaxation, their cognitive abilities become more apparent, enabling them to form more cogent judgments and thus arrive at more informed decisions.

This particular Chakra serves the purpose of mitigating the influence of superfluous and undesirable thoughts on an individual's life, enabling them to release and move on from past negative experiences. The Third Eye Chakra additionally imparts a heightened intuition regarding life's occurrences and an enhanced awareness of one's personal experiences.

The Third Eye Chakra is represented by the energies of intuition, psychic prowess, manifestation capabilities, visualizations, internal wisdom, and mental clarity. The equilibrium of the Third Eye pertains to the perceptions transcending the material plane. It implies aligning oneself with one's intuition to discern between what is morally just and unjust. It additionally fosters creativity.

The obstruction of the Third Eye can be likened to a deprivation of imaginative sight, resulting in hazy dreams and a diminished capacity for creative expression alongside a decline in intuitive prowess. The occurrence of an excessively active third eye may be infrequent due to individuals who become aware of its awakening choosing not to overtax it. Nonetheless, the manifestation of these symptoms may include experiencing hallucinations or nightmares, becoming trapped in a state of delusion, having an overly vivid imagination concerning supernatural entities, or perceiving anomalous phenomena.

Utilizing Nutritional Choices To Promote Holistic Healing: Exploring The Benefits Of The Chakra Diet

It may come as a surprise, but the dietary choices you make significantly influence not only your physical well-being but also your spiritual health. Therefore, it is imperative that you adopt the chakra diet promptly, preferably commencing today. The chakra diet is founded on the correlation between colors and distinct plant vibrations, resulting in a significantly organized approach that can be effortlessly adhered to due to its inherent color coordination. Nevertheless, numerous regulations exist, and it will become evident that the chakra diet revolves not only around what one should consume, but also what one must abstain from eating. Presented below are a few fundamental food items that you likely consume on a daily basis, which are highly recommended to be eliminated from your diet promptly.

Processed foods are the embodiment of negativity when it comes to aligning your chakras. They exhibit significantly prolonged breakdown processes within the human body, thus impeding the flow of energy through your respective portals. They induce feelings of lethargy, fatigue, and complete depletion of motivation. This exerts an unfavorable impact on your chakras, impeding the smooth circulation of energy and causing positive energy to remain externally while negative energy accumulates internally. Abstaining from the intake of processed foods will enhance your metabolism, thereby prompting the generation of a more wholesome and delightful form of energy.

• White sugar ranks prominently among the items that one should refrain from consuming. It exhibits immense addictive properties, consequently leading to significant detriment to our root and sacral chakras, not to overlook the extensive range of adverse effects on the physical well-being such as dental caries (negatively affecting the throat chakra), weight gain, and impaired circulation. Adopting a lifestyle in which you abstain from consuming refined sugar and instead obtaining your sweet cravings from natural sources can be highly beneficial for your overall well-being.

• Coffee beverage. Yes. The reliance of a vast number of individuals on this particular practice is, in fact, impeding the well-being of your chakras to a greater extent than it is benefiting them.

All forms of caffeine, including the ones present in carbonated beverages and herbal infusions, should be completely eradicated in relation to this issue. Minimal quantities of naturally occurring caffeine derived from tea are inevitable and deemed acceptable. Caffeine is classified as a stimulant substance that fails to facilitate a connection with the universe. Instead, it induces an excessive generation of deleterious emotional states such as anxiety and stress. Continual exposure to such factors has the potential to adversely affect your bodily organs, which is unequivocally unfavorable for the harmonious alignment of your chakras. Nevertheless, it is worth noting that there exist instances wherein exceptions to established patterns may arise. Occasionally, the activation of the third eye chakra may necessitate some form of stimulation. In such instances, it is permissible to consume a serving of black coffee, albeit with the aim of eventually abstaining from it in your daily routine. Use it sparingly.

• The consumption of fried foods poses significant risks to the well-being of one's chakra system. They obstruct the arterial pathways—they obstruct the energy flow through the chakras. Fried and excessively fatty foods, such as cheeseburgers, are contraindicated on the chakra diet.

• Consuming alcohol is detrimental to the balance and vitality of your warrior chakra. It leads to the exacerbation of depression and anxiety, while inducing a state of isolation that effectively disconnects you from the dynamic energy flow across all your chakras. Alcohol often elicits excessive energy and internalizes it, leading to frequent displays of aggression or anger in many instances. Experiencing intensified emotions while under the influence of alcohol can have negative effects on the balance and functioning of your chakras. The overwhelming influx of emotions in this state can cause the chakras to become overwhelmed, leading to a state of complete blockage. With that being stated, it is worth noting that alcohol may impart certain advantages when consumed in moderation, but it should never be indulged in excess. As a novice, it would be advantageous to eliminate alcohol from your lifestyle. Take the opportunity to abstain from it temporarily, and once you have achieved complete recovery, you may consider reintegrating it into your routine in moderation. However, it is crucial to exercise caution and remember that this decision is solely at your discretion.

• While drugs may not fall under the category of food in a technical sense, they are a type of consumable substance and therefore relevant to be discussed within this section of the book. The consumption of drugs is not conducive to one's well-being. The consumption of illicit drugs such as heroin, cocaine, methamphetamine, PCP, ketamine, opium, along with the misuse of prescription opiates, painkillers, and muscle relaxers, is incompatible with attaining harmonious chakras or achieving optimal mental and physical well-being. They cause extensive damage to both your mental and physical well-being and provide no assistance or benefits whatsoever. There exist shamans who endorse the utilization of potent psychoactive substances, such as mushrooms, San Pedro, DMT, and ayahuasca, and there is substantial evidence indicating the potential utility of these substances. Again, don't use them. This is an extensive journey, and the utilization of such therapeutic substances can exclusively be undertaken by an individual who possesses sound physical and mental well-being, comprehends the potential pitfalls to one's spiritual state, is proficient in remedying them, and already possesses complete knowledge encompassed within this publication. At this juncture in your life, they will bring about more adverse consequences than benefits.

Allow me to address the matter of meat. Numerous practitioners of chakra healing, spiritual leaders, traditional healers, and experienced yogis assert that the consumption of meat adversely affects the well-being and harmonious alignment of the chakra system. However, there are also numerous individuals who assert that meat consumption can effectively contribute to the restoration and harmonization of your chakras. These proponents argue that meat is occasionally essential for satisfying and fulfilling the nutritional requirements of your body. The decision of whether to include meat in your chakra diet or not rests within your personal discretion. It is an individual choice that varies among individuals, based on various reasons and personal preferences. Please be advised that if you are unfamiliar with these practices and are simultaneously adopting multiple of them—such as meditation, yoga, eliminating sugar—it is possible that transitioning to a vegetarian (or vegan) diet without prior planning may pose considerable challenges. The act of transforming one's life necessitates significant amounts of time and diligent endeavor. Therefore, it would be prudent not to allow this particular matter to be the culmination of one's hardships, particularly considering its relatively lesser significance. If you opt to exclude meat from your dietary intake, it is of utmost importance to ensure that you do so in a manner that promotes wellness, both in terms of harmonizing your chakras and maintaining your physical well-being. This necessitates ensuring an adequate intake of protein from plant-based sources, such as legumes, beans, and nuts. Should you choose to embrace a vegetarian or vegan dietary approach, it is imperative to ensure sufficient protein intake and adhere to healthy practices. Failure to do so, may result in repercussions as your chakras may become imbalanced.

If you possess the knowledge of the chakras that require extensive restoration, it is readily feasible to incorporate the chakra diet into your lifestyle. It entails incorporating an abundance of fresh produce and nutritious grains, lean proteins, and even select wholesome desserts!

If you are experiencing difficulties with your root chakra, incorporating protein into your diet is advisable. Consider consuming ample quantities of red meat and organ meat, if available. The liver greatly benefits the root chakra. Consume eggs, soy products, and nuts. Both peanut butter and almond butter exhibit desirable qualities, along with almond milk and dairy milk. Red-colored food items tend to possess beneficial properties for bolstering the functioning of the root chakra. Beets, radishes, red beans, raspberries, strawberries, tomatoes - all of these possess healing properties and attract positive energy to this location, as they align with the color red. To nourish the root chakra, incorporate an assortment of root vegetables into your diet. Potatoes, turnips, parsnips, yuca, daikon, carrots, onions, and a plethora of garlic are undoubtedly poised to provide curative effects. Consuming aromatic herbs like rosemary, chives, cayenne pepper, black pepper, horseradish, and ginger can effectively harmonize the energies of your root chakra.

In the event that you are experiencing challenges pertaining to your sacral chakra, it is advised to incorporate foods of the color orange into your diet. This particular energy center necessitates an abundant supply of sweet fruits in order to thrive and achieve optimal equilibrium. Consuming citrus fruits will prove to be highly advantageous. You require all of these citrus fruits: oranges, grapefruit, lemon, and lima. Consume fruits with higher acidity levels such as pineapple, tangerines, and mangoes. The succulent and nourishing flesh of the melon is not only a delight to taste but also offers a wealth of nutrients that benefit both the physical well-being and the vitality of the sacral energy center. Consume pumpkins, squash, carrots, sweet potatoes, and yams as they are rich in essential nutrients. Coconuts, along with almonds and walnuts, can provide assistance to you. Consume cheeses, such as cheddar and American, which possess an aesthetically pleasing orange hue. When it comes to meat, it is advisable to focus on vibrant fish varieties such as salmon and tuna to nourish this specific chakra. Consume aromatic spices such as cinnamon, caraway, fennel, anise, sesame, and vanilla bean pods in your diet. These spices can be used to create delectable beverage concoctions, which can be combined harmoniously with honey, a superlative choice of natural sweetener when adhering to the principles of the chakra diet.

The warrior chakra can be likened to a "carb" chakra, as it requires significant levels of energy to fuel its operations and achieve desired outcomes in life. Therefore, providing appropriate carbohydrates to this chakra is essential for its optimal functioning. Would you be interested in participating in the marathon? Get a promotion? It is necessary to nurture and nourish the resilience within you. Provide her (or him) with bananas, yellow lentils, bell peppers, and zucchini. The hue that emanates from the chakra of a warrior is yellow; thus, consumption of foods with a yellow hue ensures one's safety. Kindly acquire that delicious corn! Consume yellow apples and yellow pears, apricots, as well as lemons (also consider adding lemon to your tea). Consume ample amounts of yellow foods, while also incorporating a generous portion of wholesome and nutritious grains to harmonize your warrior energy center. Complete oats and oatmeal, brown rice, black rice, whole-grain varieties, bread made from nuts and seeds—these items are essential for supplying the necessary energy to support the warrior chakra. This situation presents an acceptable opportunity to audibly consume spaghetti. Please ensure you consume your pasta as well and make sure to incorporate a sufficient portion of quinoa into your diet. Dried nuts and seeds serve as a nutritious option for a snack. In addition, your warrior chakra has a strong desire for dairy products, including yellow cheeses, yogurt, and milk. Therefore, it is advisable to consume ample quantities of these items. Additionally, shellfish have positive effects on this chakra. When it comes to spices, feel free to consume cumin, ginger, turmeric, and various types of refreshing mint.

Your heart chakra requires an ample amount of love, compassion, and consumption of vegetables. This is logical, as love and kindness should originate from within one's heart, akin to the growth of spinach in the soil. Hence, it is advisable to consume ample amounts of this vegetable. Considering vegetables of green hue significantly affect the heart chakra, it is prudent to consume copious amounts of green vegetables. An assortment of nutritious leafy greens such as collard greens, kale, chard, celery, dandelion greens, and broccoli, along with a generous serving of various lettuce options, particularly romaine, are highly recommended for consumption. Consumables of a verdant hue such as cucumbers, and even pickles, are conducive to the overall well-being of the heart chakra. Consuming olives, grape leaves, and cabbage can significantly benefit cardiovascular health. Consider incorporating green tea into your beverage selection, possibly with a touch of honey if desired. Fresh verdant herbs such as jasmine, cilantro, lavender, basil, thyme, and oregano possess properties that facilitate the restoration and equilibrium of your heart chakra.

The throat chakra has a strong desire for fluids to provide relief to the throat. Freshly squeezed juices derived from the pulp of fruits are highly beneficial, particularly those that include the infusion of lemon. Attempt to craft a refreshing beverage by blending together a medley of tropical fruits such as kiwi and pineapple, along with locally-sourced berries like blueberries. The throat chakra is associated with the color blue; therefore, it is advisable to consume a variety of foods that exhibit this hue. Blue cheese and blue corn are delectable delicacies. For those who consume meat, it is advisable to select bluefin tuna and lingcod from the supermarket, given their inherent blue coloring prior to cooking. The throat chakra has a strong affinity for seaweed and kelp; hence, it is recommended to visit a nearby Japanese market and acquire these products. Consume ample quantities of teas such as chamomile and lemongrass, as well as substantial amounts of tangy fruit juices. Enhance the flavor of your culinary preparations by incorporating ingredients such as lemongrass, peppermint, and salt.

The optimal functioning of the third eye chakra necessitates the consumption of foods that are rich in darkness and sweetness. Consume foods rich in deep purples, blues, and indigos in order to nourish your pineal gland. It has a fondness for eggplant and purple chard. The third eye chakra craves the inclusion of purple kale, blueberries, and plums. This particular chakra also has an inclination towards occasionally indulging in a modest amount of dark red wine. You may also offer it a small portion of dark chocolate. This particular chakra could be considered as the "permissive" chakra, enabling the consumption of foods that might ordinarily be restricted, albeit in a manner that aligns with good health practices. The third eye chakra occasionally requires stimulation, hence, when you experience a sense of vulnerability in this domain, it would be beneficial to consume a cup of coffee as the caffeine in it will serve a positive purpose. Consume ample quantities of herbal tea and incorporate an abundance of aromatic spices into your diet, including mugwort, eyebright, lavender, poppy, and poppy seed.

The crown chakra is the focal point of transcendent spiritual connection, and therefore requires meticulous attention and care. The recommended dietary practice for this particular chakra involves abstaining from food altogether, engaging in a spiritual fast with the purpose of deepening one's connection with the universe. Numerous individuals exhibit apprehension towards fasting or harbor reservations about attempting it; nevertheless, it is highly recommended to undertake this practice. Fasting is an effective means of restoring equilibrium to all of your chakras, including those beyond the crown chakra. It alleviates the burden on your metabolic system, enabling your body to focus on its essence and its connection with the spiritual realm. The act of abstaining from food does not extend to water consumption, thus it is recommended to hydrate oneself adequately by consuming a significant amount of water—more than what may be initially perceived as necessary. Consider basking in sunlight or engaging in swimming activities, as these pursuits can effectively replenish your physical energy. In addition to water, you have the option of consuming tea or coconut juice. In the event that you choose not to abstain from food, we recommend consuming light fare such as mushrooms and coconuts. Employ traditional practices of burning and purifying herbs such as sage or palo santo, along with aromatic incense such as frankincense and myrrh, to purify your mental and physical being as well as your living space. These herbs are exclusively intended for combustion and should not be ingested.

These food items possess the potential to facilitate body detoxification and harmonization of chakras, particularly when consumed with the intent of purifying and restoring energetic balance. To adhere to the principles of the chakra diet, one must consummate their meals with mindfulness, aligning their eating habits with the way they conduct their lives. Give careful consideration to every aspect of your dietary intake. It is imperative to thoroughly review product labels before making a purchase, refraining from acquiring items that contain undesirable ingredients. Avoid procuring products that contain monosodium glutamate, corn syrup, food coloring, or any unfamiliar or unintelligible chemical components. If you possess any uncertainty, it is advisable to refrain from consuming it until thorough research has been conducted.

When considering the use of dietary supplements, it is advisable to incorporate probiotic powders, seafood powders, and fish oil into your regimen. It is crucial to conduct thorough research to ensure these supplements are free from any additional additives or substances. Ensure that the supplements you consume are of organic origin and have been meticulously manufactured.

Indeed, this statement holds true for all of your food items. It is more advantageous to consume organically grown crops, specifically vegetables and fruits. Refrain from using pesticides and any other detrimental chemical substances. Ensure that you are knowledgeable about the origins and composition of the food you consume. In the event of selecting meat for consumption, it is imperative to ensure that it has been produced and euthanized with diligent attention, while guaranteeing that the animals have not been confined within cramped facilities or feedlots. Opt for wild-caught fish rather than those that are farm-raised. All meat ought to be devoid of hormonal and antibiotic substances and derived from animals fed on a diet of grass, rather than corn or grains. Consuming food that is cultivated or harvested with conscientiousness ensures that you are acquiring a distinct form of vitality that directly transmits to your well-being.

When engaging in food preparation, establish a deliberate intention. Consuming homemade meals is significantly more conducive to maintaining one's physical and mental well-being in contrast to consuming pre-packaged or restaurant-prepared food. In the case of food prepared with love and personalized attention, such as your mother's Thanksgiving Day stuffing, it possesses inherent nourishment due to the care and affection infused into its preparation, making it a suitable exception. When embarking on the preparation of a meal, exercise discernment in your choice of ingredients, ensuring that they possess the intrinsic qualities required to align the chakras that necessitate harmonization. Please shut your eyes and conjure a mental image of your complete meal, then articulate your intention in a soft voice or silently. It may involve an activity such as aligning my sacral chakra, or another chakra. By establishing this intention, you will enhance the likelihood of achieving your desired outcomes and foster a positive and constructive energy that will contribute to the realization of your intent. Similarly, should you opt to engage in fasting, it is advisable to establish a purpose or objective for doing so. Employing fasting is akin to utilizing food as a means to harmonize one's chakras, albeit with the caveat that fasting should not be practiced on a daily basis. Incorporate meditation extensively during your fasting regime to harness the advantageous outcomes stemming from your disciplined restraint.

The Practice Of Mindfulness And Balancing The Body's Energy Centers Through Meditation

As you cultivate a state of increased calmness in your respiration, it becomes beneficial to initiate the practice of envisioning and focusing on each individual chakra. You aim to perceptually depict the flow of energy within each chakra. This may pose a slight difficulty for beginners. Be patient with yourself. It is permissible for your attention to occasionally divert. When such instances occur, it is imperative to recognize any distraction that has captured your mental focus, and subsequently release it. Reorient your attention to your breath as necessary, and subsequently redirect your focus towards the movement of energy within your chakras.

Direct your attention to each individual chakra, starting with the root chakra and ascending to the crown chakra. Picture the energy in each chakra. Allocate a few minutes of focused concentration to each individual chakra. Direct your attention to the hue corresponding to each chakra. Envision the dynamic flow of energy, causing the colors to transform correspondingly in accordance with the chakra it is traversing. Observe the upward movement of energy, halting at every chakra to illuminate it. Maintain your focus on the chakra until its hue becomes exceedingly vibrant and luminous. The ultimate objective is to cultivate a vivid mental visualization of the harmonious flow of positive energy within your being.

Engage in meditation with a receptive mindset and a modest attitude. The state of enlightenment, attained through the practice of meditation, is a recurrent occurrence observed among individuals from diverse backgrounds. Although these experiences may not be regarded as miraculous by others, they were deemed miraculous by the individuals who had the privilege of experiencing them. Therefore, approach the practice of meditation with the ultimate objective of facilitating the free flow of energy and observe the path it leads you towards.

The chakras represent a crucial equilibrium that pervades the entire human body. In the event that one of the elements becomes misaligned or experiences an obstruction hindering its ability to receive the necessary energy, it should become apparent which specific element is affected. Once you have developed a deeper familiarity with the chakras and their respective positions within the body, you will acquire the ability to discern potential obstructions based on the physiological reactions you might experience during the act of breathing. Maintain an awareness of the inherent energy dynamics within your body during the process of inhalation and exhalation. Initially, this may provoke uneasiness and necessitate a significant amount of devoted effort. Have faith in the innate wisdom of your energy and physical being to signal any necessary advancements or enhancements.

Upon concluding your meditation session, should you sense a heightened awareness of the areas wherein you encounter difficulties, it would be beneficial to make a written record of your observations for future reference. Subsequently, you may endeavor to incorporate certain activities into your daily routine with the intention of facilitating the healing process of these specific chakras. There exist a few uncomplicated exercises that one can engage in to achieve the objective of aligning and expanding the chakras.

The primary chakra, known as the root chakra, requires a sense of safety and security. It may be beneficial for your meditation practice to consider incorporating a mantra while assuming the appropriate physical posture. "I am safe. I am secure. I have been confined to my residence.

The sacral chakra, which pertains to emotions, requires conscious inhalation and exhalation as well as affirmations of emotional stability. Having inspirational quotes displayed in your home can serve as a reminder of your emotional agency, thereby potentially aiding you in moments of introspection.

The solar plexus chakra – If you perceive a difficulty in effectively communicating your thoughts or realizing that you have exhibited excessive discourtesy towards others, it is plausible that there exists an obstruction within this particular region. This chakra governs the profound emotions of self-love and self-acceptance. Strive to cultivate contentment with your individual identity and exhibit benevolence towards those in your vicinity.

The cardiac chakra - Welcome the world with tranquility and affection. A pleasant demeanor towards the world often elicits a reciprocated positive response. You inhibit the flow of this chakra through your inability to articulate expressions of affection. Merely by altering one's perspective, it is possible to facilitate the unblocking of this chakra, thereby allowing the smooth passage of energy.

The throat chakra can be influenced by your bodily alignment. Does your head experience a satisfactory level of comfort while you sleep? To what extent do you regularly engage in vocalizing audibly? Endeavor to attempt it, whether it be solely within the confines of the bathing enclosure. The activity in which you are engaging is initiating the opening process of this chakra. Additionally, maintaining a proper posture with a slightly lowered head is beneficial during the practice of meditation.

The levels of concentration and the degree of discipline exerted during meditation have an impact on the third eye chakra and the Crown Chakra. Nonetheless, there are alternative means through which one can cultivate mental discipline, thus facilitating the opening of these respective regions. As an illustration, the practice of mindfulness serves as a prime example in this regard. This is the point at which you can discern which elements pertain to the past or the future, as well as those that pertain to the current present moment. It is only this moment in time that matters. All alternate thoughts are futile. Engage in the exercise of redirecting your thought patterns to the present moment and eliminating any debilitating thoughts that impede your quest for enlightenment. Reflections on prior experiences will perpetually impede the alignment of the chakras, particularly fixating on past relationships well beyond their termination. Embrace a joyous disposition towards life in order to facilitate the healing of these chakras.

Exercise caution regarding any emotions and thoughts that arise during the course of this procedure. On certain occasions, one might encounter moments of profound insight, while on others, memories of a distressing nature may resurface. It constitutes an integral aspect of the therapeutic process involving meditation. Simply bear in mind to refrain from fixating on these thoughts. Recognize their presence and subsequently let them go. When one permits ruminations of the past to impede progress, the process of attaining emotional or physical recovery becomes arduous. Once you release your grip on them, there is no cause for trepidation. Frequently, individuals hesitate to relinquish these thoughts and memories as they perceive them to be integral components of their identity. To a certain extent, this claim holds validity. However, if one refuses to relinquish one's grip, progress will remain elusive, thus impeding the process of personal healing. Mastering the art of relinquishment poses great challenges to individuals unacquainted with the act, yet engaging in meditative exercises on a regular basis, allocating approximately 20 minutes each day, has the potential to significantly alter cognitive processes.

Following your session, it is recommended that you make written notes outlining the issues or topics that you wish to discuss in the subsequent session. On occasion, it may be beneficial to render a visual representation of your chakras by means of a diagram, and subsequently annotate any obstructions you may be encountering in close proximity to each respective chakra. By engaging in this practice, you will have the opportunity to review your thoughts and experiences prior to commencing your subsequent session of meditation.

Chapter Three - The Functioning Mechanism of Chakras

What is the philosophical concept behind the Chakras? Chakras are commonly referred to as energy centers and are known to be imperceptible to the naked eye. The observation of the chakras is contingent upon their functioning. Highly skilled and enthusiastic professionals have the capability to effortlessly perceive these centers, just as if they were directly gazing upon them. Similarly, individuals who possess a genuine ardor for the subject and invest substantial effort into honing their abilities can achieve the same level of observation. Despite the absence of tangible manifestations, chakras possess the capacity to directly impact the functioning of the human body. As previously indicated, they exert a direct influence not solely on your physical well-being, but also on your emotional and spiritual states. To facilitate a harmonious existence, it is imperative to harmonize the chakras, as their disharmony significantly disrupts the equilibrium of one's life. The optimal functioning of Chakras hinges on their state of equilibrium. If they are in equilibrium, it signifies that they are functioning as intended. Under normal circumstances, the Chakras facilitate a seamless and unobstructed movement of energy within our physiological system, ensuring a continuous and uninhibited revitalization process. This energy serves as a means of establishing a connection with the entirety, enabling us to establish connections with its various constituent parts. This enables us to effectively communicate and comprehend the underlying significance of our existence. However, in instances where there is an imbalance in the

Chakras, the natural flow of energy encounters hindrance and obstruction. This phenomenon gives rise to disturbances in both physical and mental well-being. Chakras are commonly perceived as swirling structures, and in order to comprehend their nature, a novice can draw a parallel between them and the aperture at the base of the sink. When the drain orifice is unobstructed, the water is capable of unhindered evacuation from the sink; however, in the event of any hindrance, the regular flow of water is disrupted, resulting in stagnation and the accumulation of impurities. The stagnant water exerts pressure on the sink, resulting in its damage. The Influence of Chakras on Various Facets of Existence There have been references to seven fundamental chakras in the preceding chapter, each of which holds correlation with specific domains of an individual's life. This principle is fundamentally elementary, and its prompt comprehension can prove advantageous for individuals. Regardless of personal belief in this notion, it relies entirely on rational thinking. Engaging in an inquiry into how each chakra influences specific facets of one's life can be a constructive and advantageous pursuit, fostering self-awareness by revealing perceived inadequacies in one's character. Upon acquiring comprehension of the issue at hand, one gains the capability to devise exemplary and highly efficient resolutions. Presented below is a concise overview delineating the various spheres of existence that are impacted by each individual chakra within the framework of the 7 fundamental energy centers.

- The Root Chakra influences one's instinct for survival and the manner in which they establish a connection with the physical realm. In instances of hypoactivity, individuals may experience perpetual nervousness, a sense of displacement, and chronic insecurity. When in a state of heightened activity, it has a tendency to incite avarice, foster an inclination for excessive control, and engender a preoccupation with material possessions.
- The Sacral Chakra is responsible for governing an individual's

emotions and desires related to intimacy and sexuality. In a passive state, an individual exhibits a tendency to isolate themselves from social interactions, confining themselves to their own isolated reality. Consequently, such individuals encounter challenges when attempting to articulate their emotions. In the event that the sacral chakra is excessively stimulated, it can result in an individual experiencing heightened emotional sensitivity and a constant state of near outbursts. Additionally, it surpasses the acceptable threshold of sexual desire. • The Solar Plexus Chakra governs an individual's self-assurance and capacity to assert themselves. The suboptimal functioning of the third chakra is associated with manifestations of ambiguity, indecisiveness, and diminished self-esteem. When in a state of heightened activity, this chakra induces an individual to display an assertive and authoritative demeanor which permeates various facets of their existence. • The Heart Chakra is responsible for regulating the qualities of empathy and affection. The emotions of empathy and compassion towards others are similarly associated with the heart chakra. An obstructed Heart Chakra can lead to an individual displaying a significant lack of empathy or concern towards the emotions and well-being of those in their vicinity, often exhibiting a cold and indifferent demeanor. When experiencing excessive levels of attention and concern for others, an individual can become burdensome to those around them, leading people to feel compelled to distance themselves from this person in order to avoid feeling overwhelmed.

• Throat Chakra

The throat chakra encompasses an individual's capacity for communication, encompassing their ability to effectively express ideas and emotions to others. In instances where an individual's throat chakra becomes obstructed, it is not uncommon for them to display a proclivity towards reticence and introversion. Individuals lacking the capacity to attentively heed others and those who endeavor to impose their viewpoints in dialogue without comprehending the perspectives of others often exhibit an excessively engaged Throat Chakra. • The Third Eye encompasses cognitive elements pertaining to an individual, including the capacity to envision diverse concepts and scenarios, unrestricted and imaginative thinking, and profound discernment. Individuals who exhibit diminished levels of engagement in the Third Eye demonstrate characteristics such as rigid and superficial thought processes, frequently relying excessively on external influences. Elevated Third Eye activity results in an individual venturing into the realm of their own imagination, and in severe instances, these imaginative constructs can escalate into manifestations of delusional perceptions. • The Crown: The faculties of cognition, the transcendental essence, and the existential alignment are the dimensions of your existence that are influenced by the Crown. When one experiences an abnormally diminished level of activity in the realm of authority, their awareness of the spiritual facets of existence becomes obscured. When the monarchy displays excessive activity, individuals tend to disregard their physical needs and deviate from rationality and sound judgment.

Chapter 3 – Exploring the Integration of the Following Three Chakras

In numerous aspects, while being crucial for proper growth and remarkably effective, the initial three chakras predominantly revolve around self-centeredness. During the initial stages of development and potentially extending up until early adolescence, this particular concentration does not result in catastrophic consequences. However, as an individual progresses in age, it is imperative that their attention shifts beyond themselves and simultaneously grows in intensity.

This is the point at which the heart chakra is implicated. The heart chakra serves as the domicile of profound sentiments. The hue of this item is either a delicate shade of pink or a vibrant, pristine green, while it goes by the name Anahata. It transcends mere sensuality to establish a profound connection with an individual sharing similar thoughts and passions.

It embodies the fervor of an artist, the unwavering commitment of a genuine humanitarian, and the boundless affection bestowed upon a child or a life partner. When the equilibrium of this chakra is attained, individuals experience a sense of unity, fulfillment, vitality, self-assurance, and display affectionate and merciful traits.

Merely possessing emotions falls short in terms of fostering successful interpersonal relationships and effectively addressing external circumstances. In order to achieve goals and aspirations, it is imperative to impart and disseminate the emotions, commitment, and concentration to others.

This is the point at which the throat chakra, known as Vishuddha, comes into play. It regulates the faculty of verbal communication and the transmission of thoughts and concepts to individuals; conversely, it also assumes the responsibility for the capacity to attentively perceive and understand the meaning conveyed by others. The hues of this entity consist of vivid shades of blue, reminiscent of the expansive ocean or a crystal-clear summer sky. When there is an equilibrium, it becomes effortless to communicate significance to others and to comprehend it in return.

The Brow Chakra, also known as the third eye, is designated by the name Anja. It is widely regarded as the bastion of erudition, comprehension, and innate insight. In certain frameworks, it is postulated that it confers the capacity to perceive auras and comprehend individuals on a profound level. It oversees the functioning of the nervous system and contributes to the formation of innovative ideas and breakthroughs across various academic and professional domains.

Beginners frequently overlook the fact that the energies flow through all the chakras, placing excessive emphasis on these three upper chakras. For the system to function optimally, it is necessary that all components maintain equilibrium and collaborate harmoniously.

In the Occidental realm, dating back to the early medieval era, a proclivity has emerged to diminish the significance attributed to the tangible world and instead direct contemplation towards a transcendent entity. Although not entirely incorrect, it has regrettably resulted in the overlooking, or even suppression, of natural processes in order to prioritize spiritual concerns.

Although it may be commendable to prioritize one's spiritual well-being, disregarding the maintenance of the lower chakras can lead to undesirable outcomes. Consider, if you will, the endeavor of attempting to maintain equilibrium of a pyramid atop its apex, rather than the stable foundation provided by its broad base.

This will provide you with a comprehensive understanding of the challenges associated with adopting a hierarchical approach to the study and development of the chakras. Alternatively, one could contemplate Maslow's pyramid of human needs as an alternative means of expressing the same idea. He expressed that prioritizing the fulfillment of fundamental needs, prior to addressing the more intangible ones, yields diminishing efficacy.

www.ingramcontent.com/pod-product-compliance
Lightning Source LLC
Chambersburg PA
CBHW050247120526
44590CB00016B/2255